★ It's My State! ★ ★ ★ ★

WASHINGTON

The Evergreen State

Steven Otfinoski, Tea Benduhn, and Hex Kleinmartin

Cavendish Square

New York

Published in 2015 by Cavendish Square Publishing, LLC
243 5th Avenue, Suite 136, New York, NY 10016

Copyright © 2015 by Cavendish Square Publishing, LLC

First Edition

Website: cavendishsq.com

This publication represents the opinions and views of the author based on his or her personal experience, knowledge, and research. The information in this book serves as a general guide only. The author and publisher have used their best efforts in preparing this book and disclaim liability rising directly or indirectly from the use and application of this book.

CPSIA Compliance Information: Batch #WW15CSQ

All websites were available and accurate when this book was sent to press.

Library of Congress Cataloging-in-Publication Data

Kleinmartin, Hex.
Washington / by Hex Kleinmartin, Steven Otfinoski, and Tea Benduhn — third edition.
p. cm. — (It's my state!)
Includes index.
ISBN 978-1-50260-007-3 (hardcover) ISBN 978-1-50260-008-0 (ebook)
1. Washington (State) — Juvenile literature. I. Kleinmartin, Hex. II. Altman, Linda Jacobs, 1943- III. Benduhn, Tea. IV. Title.
F891.3 K54 2015
979.7—d23

Editor: Fletcher Doyle
Senior Copy Editor: Wendy A. Reynolds
Art Director: Jeffrey Talbot
Designer: Joseph Macri
Senior Production Manager: Jennifer Ryder-Talbot
Production Editor: David McNamara
Photo Research by J8 Media

Printed in the United States of America

WASHINGTON
CONTENTS

A QUICK LOOK AT

⭐ State Flower: Coast Rhododendron

The name rhododendron means "rose tree," and the plant's beautiful flowers grow in clusters. Rhododendrons have large, shiny evergreen leaves that are poisonous when eaten. The coast rhododendron was chosen as Washington's state flower in 1892.

⭐ State Bird: Willow Goldfinch

The goldfinch is a small bird with yellow markings and black wings. It is sometimes called the wild canary because of its sweet song. The goldfinch's cup-shaped nest can hold water because it is built so tightly.

⭐ State Tree: Western Hemlock

Washington's early residents used the western hemlock's reddish-brown bark for tanning leather and dyeing objects. A type of pine tree that can grow as tall as 200 feet (60 meters), its wood was used to carve cooking utensils and other tools.

WASHINGTON

★ State Marine Mammal: Orca

The orca (also known as the killer whale) belongs to the oceanic dolphin family. This species has a diverse diet, although individual populations often specialize in particular types of prey. Some feed exclusively on fish, while others hunt marine mammals.

★ State Gem: Petrified Wood

Petrified wood was created millions of years ago in Washington's swampy interior. Water seeped into the trees, and minerals in the water gradually replaced the wood. Eventually, these substances hardened, and the wood turned to stone.

★ State Fish: Steelhead Trout

A Steelhead trout can be silver-gray with spots along its back, while some have pinkish red colorings, and others have white bellies. Born in fresh water, the trout travels to the ocean's salt waters. As an adult it returns to freshwater streams and rivers to breed.

Ferries reduce travel time in the communities around Puget Sound.

The Evergreen State

Washington is the only state in the nation named for a president: George Washington. The nation's capital is called Washington, D.C., so the state is often called Washington State to avoid confusion. Like the first president, Washington is first in many things, such as the production of apples and sweet cherries and the **manufacturing** of airplanes and other technology products.

Washington is located in the northwestern corner of the contiguous, or connected, forty-eight U.S. states. The state's northern, eastern, and southeastern borders are fairly straight (except where the Snake River makes up the southernmost part of the eastern border). The southwestern border, which follows the Columbia River, is much more irregular in shape, as is the western border, which is the coast of the Pacific Ocean. Washington is the smallest of the three contiguous states bordering the Pacific Ocean (the others are Oregon and California). Containing thirty-nine counties, the state has a land area of 66,544 square miles (172,348 square kilometers), making it the twentieth-largest state in the country in land area.

The Landscape

Washington's mountains, valleys, and waterways were formed over the course of millions of years. **Glaciers**, or slow-moving ice masses, created some of the land features. Volcanic

Palouse Falls State Park is in the Columbia Plateau, located in the region east of the Cascades.

State Borders

North: Canada

South: Oregon

East: Idaho

West: Pacific Ocean

eruptions and land erosion are other factors that altered the surface of the land. The shape and surface of the land have also been affected by the movement of large slabs of rock found beneath Earth's surface called tectonic plates. The movement of plates causes mountain ranges, earthquakes, and volcanic eruptions.

Three major mountain ranges cross through Washington. The Rocky Mountains extend from Canada down to northern New Mexico. A portion of the Rockies stretches across the northeastern corner of Washington. This portion is sometimes called the Selkirk Mountains. The types of animals and plants that live in some parts of the Rockies, such as at high elevations, are very different from the types that live in other areas.

The Olympic Mountains are located in the northwestern section of the state. These coastal mountains cover approximately 3,500 square miles (9,000 sq. km). The highest peak in this mountain range is Mount Olympus, which is about 7,965 feet (2,428 m) high. A large part of the range is located in Olympic National Park. The park has rain forests as well. Rain and fertile soil make the area perfect for trees such as spruce, hemlock, cedars, and firs, as well as for other plants, including moss. Elk, bears, deer, and mountain lions roam parts of the park.

The Cascade Range is found between the Rockies and the Olympic Mountains. The mountains of the Cascades run from north to south and divide the state almost in half. The Cascades contain Mount Rainier, the tallest peak in the state at 14,410 feet (4,392 m).

In 1980, Mount St. Helens erupted, literally blowing its top—the volcano lost more than 1,300 feet (400 m) of its height, dropping it from being the fifth highest peak in the state to the thirteenth. This opened a crater, sending hot ash raining down that destroyed crops and wildlife. The heat caused the surrounding snow to melt, which resulted in flooding and mud slides. The volcanic explosions were so strong that they knocked down tens of thousands of acres of trees. Since the 1980 eruption, wildlife has flourished again, and communities have been rebuilt. Mount St. Helens erupted again in 2004, but that eruption was not as destructive. Lava pierced the crater floor, and the volcano erupted continually until 2008, building a new lava dome.

Volcanic eruptions that occurred thousands of years ago helped to create the region east of the Cascades, called the Columbia Plateau. The Columbia Plateau is raised up because of hardened lava that flowed from the volcanic eruptions. Cities such as Spokane, Walla Walla, and Yakima are located on the plateau. The Yakima, Columbia, and Spokane rivers flow through the area, and the land around those rivers tends to be fertile and ideal for growing crops, such as wheat.

Washington Waterways

Washington has many bodies of water flowing into, out of, and across the state. A long arm of water called the Strait of Juan de Fuca leads from the Pacific Ocean into Puget Sound. The sound was created thousands of years ago when glaciers moved through the

WASHINGTON
COUNTY MAP

WHATCOM

SAN JUAN
ISLAND

SKAGIT

OKANOGAN

FERRY

STEVENS

PEND
OREILLE

CLALLAM

SNOHOMISH

CHELAN

DOUGLAS

LINCOLN

SPOKANE

JEFFERSON

KITSAP

MASON

KING

GRAYS
HARBOR

KITTITAS

GRANT

ADAMS

WHITMAN

THURSTON

PIERCE

PACIFIC

LEWIS

YAKIMA

FRANKLIN

GARFIELD

WAHKIAKUM

COLUMBIA

COWLITZ

SKAMANIA

BENTON

WALLA WALLA

ASOTIN

CLARK

KLICKITAT

WASHINGTON
POPULATION BY COUNTY

County	Population	County	Population
Adams County	18,728	San Juan County	15,769
Asotin County	21,623	Skagit County	116,901
Benton County	175,177	Skamania County	11,066
Chelan County	72,453	Snohomish County	713,335
Clallam County	71,404	Spokane County	471,221
Clark County	425,363	Stevens County	43,531
Columbia County	4,078	Thurston County	252,264
Cowlitz County	102,410	Wahkiakum County	3,978
Douglas County	38,431	Walla Walla County	58,781
Ferry County	7,551	Whatcom County	201,140
Franklin County	78,163	Whitman County	44,776
Garfield County	2,266	Yakima County	243,231
Grant County	89,120		
Grays Harbor County	72,797		
Island County	78,506		
Jefferson County	29,872		
King County	1,931,249		
Kitsap County	251,133		
Kittitas County	40,915		
Klickitat County	20,318		
Lewis County	75,455		
Lincoln County	10,570		
Mason County	60,699		
Okanogan County	41,120		
Pacific County	20,920		
Pend Oreille County	13,001		
Pierce County	795,225		

Source: U.S. Bureau of the Census, 2010

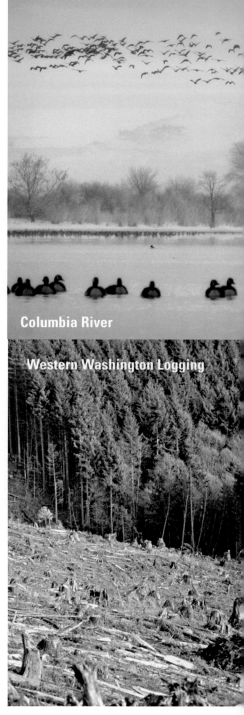

Columbia River

Western Washington Logging

Dams along the Columbia River help generate one-third of all hydroelectric power in the United States.

area and carved up the land. Most of the state's **population** lives in the area around Puget Sound. Three of the state's major cities—Seattle, Tacoma, and the capital, Olympia—are near the sound.

Puget Sound is also home to many islands. Bainbridge Island is just a ferry ride away from Seattle. The San Juan Islands attract visitors who enjoy activities such as hiking, sailing, scuba diving, and exploring the state parks. Residents of the islands create their own thriving communities.

The state also has many rivers, streams, and lakes. The Puyallup River flows past Tacoma into Puget Sound. Other rivers, such as the Quinault, flow into the Pacific Ocean.

The longest river in Washington is the Columbia. It begins in British Columbia and cuts down through the middle of Washington. At the south end of the state, the river heads westward and forms much of the border between Washington and Oregon before emptying into the Pacific Ocean. The Snake River, Lewis River, Spokane River, Klickitat River, and Cowlitz River all flow into the Columbia River. Washington has harnessed the power of the Columbia River with human-made **dams** that control flooding and create electricity, and water from the reservoirs that form behind the dams is used to irrigate farmland. The dams were built to control the river, but as a result, other areas were permanently flooded when the reservoirs were created. The dams also affect the migration of some types of fish, especially salmon.

There are more than one thousand natural lakes in Washington. The largest natural lake is Lake Chelan, located in the central region. The state has larger lakes, but they are reservoirs created by dams. Lake Roosevelt, the largest such lake, is more than 150 miles (240 km) long. It was named for President Franklin D. Roosevelt.

Climate

Thanks to the moist air blowing in from the Pacific Ocean, Washington's western coast has mild winters and cool summers. No other part of the United States that far north has such warm winter weather. The ocean winds also contain lots of moisture that turns into rain. The region gets rain an average of 150 to 180 days a year and has areas of rain forest. The region also gets some snow in the wintertime. Mount Baker, which is near Bellingham, holds the record for the heaviest winter snowfall in the country. In 1999, an amazing 95 feet (29 m) of snow fell.

Mount Baker is one of the snowiest spots in the United States.

Columbia Gorge Riverboat

Mount Rainier

Mount St. Helens

1. Columbia Gorge Riverboat

Learn about the Columbia River Gorge and the Lewis and Clark Expedition during a two-hour narrated cruise out of Vancouver. The 147-foot (45 m) sternwheeler is patterned after a nineteenth century steamer, designed to slide over the Columbia River's sandbars.

2. Coulee Corridor, Including Grand Coulee Dam

The Coulee Corridor National Scenic Byway runs from Omak in the north, through Moses Lake, to Othello. Dry Falls Interpretive Center, Steamboat Rock State Park, and Potholes State Park are also great places to learn about the area.

3. Fort Nisqually Living History Museum

Tacoma's Fort Nisqually was the first European settlement on Puget Sound and a bustling center of trade that expanded into a large-scale agricultural enterprise. Discover what life was like in the 1850s at the region's premier living history museum.

4. Mount Rainier National Park

The stunning beauty and dominant presence of Mount Rainier National Park can be experienced on a driving tour with frequent stops at scenic viewpoints, or hikes that range from easy to difficult.

5. Mount St. Helens National Volcanic Monument

Getting up close to an active volcano provides a certain thrill. By driving through Mount St. Helens National Monument, one can see evidence of the vast destruction from the 1980 eruption and signs of amazing recovery in plant and animal life.

WASHINGTON

6. Olympic National Park

Olympic National Park is a unique and diverse wilderness preserve where you can experience a number of different ecosystems, including alpine mountain, temperate rain forests, and rugged ocean beaches. The park provides a home for the largest unmanaged herd of Roosevelt elk in the world.

7. Pike Place Market

Seattle's Pike Place Market is packed full of more stalls, shops, and eateries than you can explore in just one visit. A gorgeous array of seafood, produce, and flowers makes the Market a favorite with both visitors and residents.

8. Riverfront Park

World's fairs and expositions have left Washington with wonderful community spaces and unique structures that have gone on to become treasured landmarks. Expo '74 transformed Spokane's downtown railroad yards into lovely green spaces dotted with interesting buildings.

9. Seattle Center

A legacy of the 1962 Century 21 Exposition, Seattle Center combines open park spaces with a number of attractions and performance venues. Many of Seattle's major annual festivals are held at Seattle Center.

10. Washington State Ferries

Not only are the Washington State Ferries often the only way to get to the many island communities scattered around the Puget Sound, they are also a fun and relaxing way to experience the beauty of the region.

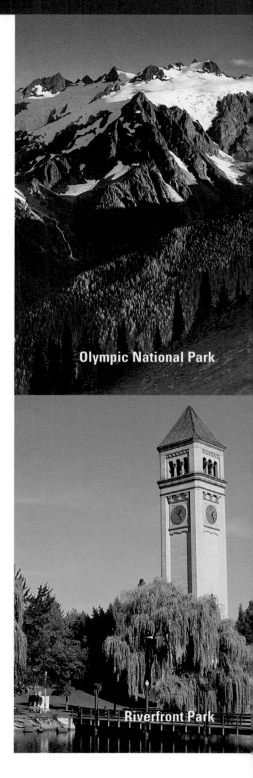

Olympic National Park

Riverfront Park

The Cascade Range tends to block the warm and moist Pacific air from reaching eastern Washington, giving that part of the state a different **climate**. The winters are usually very cold and the summers are hot. The temperatures can go well below 0 degrees Fahrenheit (–18 degrees Celsius) in the winter and above 100°F (38°C) in the summer. Rainfall is not as heavy in this part of the state. Some parts of the eastern region average only about 6 inches (15 cm) of rain each year.

Life in the Wild

Washington's thick forests are home to tall Douglas fir, Sitka spruce, and western hemlock, the state tree. Some of the trees are hundreds of years old. Cottonwood, maple, and ash trees dot the state's lush green forests. Lodgepole pines and western larch grow tall in the less-wooded eastern region. Warm areas of the state have different types of mosses and ferns.

Trees in Washington's thick forests can live for hundreds of years.

Hikers see stunning views in North Cascades National Park.

Wildflowers thrive in the mild, wet climate of Puget Sound. Fields and meadows are bright with brown- and black-eyed Susans, lupine, goldenrod, and Indian paintbrush. Coast rhododendron, the state flower, covers hillsides and slopes in the Cascades' foothills.

Washington's forests and marshes are filled with small animals. These include beavers, minks, muskrats, and marmots. Larger animals, such as mountain lions, mountain goats, and coyotes, can also be found in different parts of the state. Many types of deer call Washington home. They include the elk and the mule deer.

Throughout the state, lakes and rivers are filled with whitefish, giant sturgeon, and several kinds of trout. The offshore waters of the Pacific swarm with seals, porpoises, salmon, and some of the largest octopuses found anywhere in the world. Orcas and gray whales can be seen traveling along the coast.

Bald eagles and cranes are just two of the birds that can be found in the state. Flocks of pelicans, puffins, seagulls, and oystercatchers fly above the state's waters. Washington's temperate rain forests also have spotted owls, flycatchers, and crossbills.

Douglas Fir

Harbor Seal

Lupine

1. Beaver

Beavers are the largest rodents in North America, with adults averaging 40 pounds (18 kg) and measuring more than 3 feet (1 m) long, including the tail. These semi-aquatic mammals have webbed hind feet, large incisor teeth, and a broad, flat tail.

2. Douglas Fir

This tall evergreen tree can grow as high as 250 feet (76 m). The tallest one, found near Little Rock, was 330 feet (100 m) tall. The average life span of a Douglas fir is 500 years, though it can live for up to 1,000.

3. Harbor Seal

Many harbor seals enjoy basking on the large rocks and beaches along Puget Sound. They may grow to be 7 feet (2.1 m) long and can weigh more than 200 pounds (90.7 kg). Their diet includes fish and squid.

4. Lupine

A member of the pea family, the lupine plant has clusters of colorful flowers. Lupine can be pink, blue, white, or a mixture of these colors. There are around one hundred kinds of lupine in the United States and Canada.

5. Mule Deer

The mule deer got its name from its long, furry ears, which resemble a mule's. It is also known for the unusually stiff way it walks. Its diet consists of grass and the twigs, leaves, and buds of shrubs.

6. Orca

Also known as the killer whale, the orca is around 30 feet (9 m) long. Orcas often hunt in packs and prey upon fish, seals, and even whales. Scientists study them in the open sea and in coastal waters.

7. Oystercatcher

This black bird gets its name from its favorite food—oysters. It lives on the shore and uses its long, red-orange bill to pry open the shells of oysters. Oystercatchers lay their eggs on the rocks on the shore.

8. Postelsia

Postelsia, also known as the sea palm or palm seaweed, is found along the western coast of North America, on rocky shores with constant waves. While it was eaten by Native Americans, it is now illegal to harvest.

9. Rainbow Trout

Rainbow trout is the most common freshwater fish. It is a species of salmonid native to cold-water tributaries, with adult freshwater stream rainbow trout averaging between 1 and 5 pounds (0.5 and 2.3 kg). Lake-dwelling forms may reach 20 lb. (9.1 kg).

10. Western Redcedar

Western redcedar is among the most widespread trees in the Pacific Northwest and is valued for its appearance, aroma, and its high natural resistance to decay. Many native groups used it to build houses and canoes, and even to make clothes.

Oystercatcher

Western Redcedar

Life could be hard in logging camps in the 1920s.

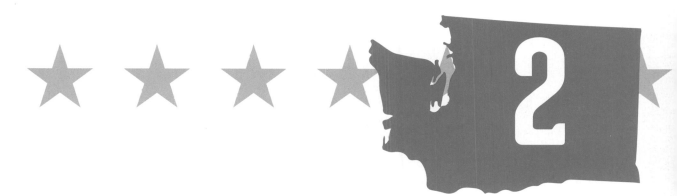

From the Beginning

Present-day Washington was once, in the words of one visitor, a "remote and savage" land. It was one of the last regions of the forty-eight contiguous states to be thoroughly explored. Once people saw the riches of this wilderness, however, growth was rapid. The population has been growing ever since.

Washington's Native Peoples arrived at least 12,000 years ago across a land bridge that connected North America with Asia. This bridge was exposed by the lower sea levels that existed during the Ice Age. People from Asia crossed over the land bridge and eventually spread out and settled in different parts of North America.

The First Explorers

For two hundred years, explorers traveled to what is now Washington only from the sea. Greek explorer Juan de Fuca claimed to have sailed along the region's shore in 1592. The Strait of Juan de Fuca, leading into Puget Sound, is named for him. British captain George Vancouver retraced his route two hundred years later and sailed into Puget Sound. He and his men explored the islands of the sound. That same year, American captain Robert Gray sailed into the mouth of the Columbia River. He sailed up the river and named it after his ship, the Columbia. Both the British and the Americans claimed the region.

In November 1805, the American explorers Meriwether Lewis and William Clark reached the Pacific Ocean at the mouth of the Columbia River. They had traveled all the way from St. Louis to explore the Louisiana Purchase (a huge territory between the Mississippi River and the Rocky Mountains that the United States had bought from France in 1803) and to find a water route to the Pacific Ocean. During their travels, they made contact with Native Americans who aided them in their journey. Lewis and Clark's celebrated expedition strengthened the United States' claim to the Pacific Northwest.

American, Canadian, and British traders soon arrived in the region. They wanted to trade with the Native Americans. One of the main items these traders wanted was furs. Hats and other goods made out of fur and leather were popular at the time. Many Native Americans traded these animal skins for tools, knives, and other American or British goods.

Lewis and Clark received help from Native Americans on their trip from St. Louis to the Pacific Ocean.

Fort Okanogan was established to expand the fur trade.

During the early 1800s, American John Jacob Astor established different sites—or outposts—for fur trading. The outposts around the Columbia River Valley were part of his Pacific Fur Company. In 1811, an outpost named Fort Okanogan was established at the junction of the Okanogan and Columbia rivers. Today, Fort Okanogan State Park overlooks the site of the fort. The park includes a museum with exhibits about the fur trading **industry**.

Ice Covered

There are more glaciers in the state of Washington than in the other forty-seven contiguous states combined.

In 1818, the United States and Great Britain agreed to share the region they called the Oregon Country. This area included the present-day states of Oregon, Washington and Idaho, parts of present-day Montana and Wyoming, and much of the present-day Canadian province of British Columbia. In 1824, Fort Vancouver was established by a British trader named John McLoughlin. Located on the Columbia River, it became the biggest and most important community in what is now Washington.

The Native People

When European explorers arrived, the tribes of what is now Washington were separated geographically into two main groups: those that lived west of the Cascade Mountains and those that lived east of the mountains. Those that lived west of the Cascades included the Chehalis, Chinook, Clatsop, Lummi, Klalam, Nooksack, Puyallup, Quinault, Quileaute, Skagit, Snohomish, Snoqualmie, Swinomish, and Tulalip. Those east of the mountain range included the Cayuse, Coeur D'Alene, Colville, Interior Salish, Kalispel, Makah, Nez Perce, Palouse, Salish, Spokane, Umatilla, and Yakima.

They lived very different lives. The region east of the Cascades is drier with greater weather extremes than on the other side. Tribes there often lived in pit houses. They had a living space dug from the ground with a dome-shaped wooden frame, packed with earth, built over it. These homes were about 15 feet (4.6 m) across and held only one family. They gathered roots, berries, and other plants, and also fished and hunted. Some were nomadic, following the animals they were hunting. They would use tepees while on the move, like the Plains Indians. Those in the coastal areas lived in permanent homes of cedar wood. They ate more seafood and less of the plant and land animals that the inland natives ate. They made canoes dug out from cedar logs, and hunted seals, sea lions, and even whales from them.

The opening of the Oregon Trail brought **settlers** and led to wars over the possession of land. The tribes of this region suffered mostly from epidemics of diseases such as smallpox, which were present even before the arrival of the explorers Lewis and Clark in 1805. The tribes along the Columbia River were particularly hard hit.

These tepees belong to the Colville, a tribe that lived east of the Cascades.

The tribes were moved off their land onto **reservations** but they weren't sent nearly as far as the Native groups in the eastern United States. That is why Washington has one of the largest native populations in the United States. It is one of fourteen states with more than 100,000 indigenous residents. There are twenty-nine federally recognized tribes in Washington today.

Spotlight on The Makah

Historically, the Makah tribe has been relatively small, with five villages in existence at the same time. They built canoes of cedar, made fishhooks from roots, bones, sinew, and twine, and wove baskets from bear grass and cedar bark.

Distribution: Currently, the Makah occupy a reservation of 122 square kilometers (47 sq. mi) on the most northwestern tip of the Olympic Peninsula in Clallam County. The group has about 1,400 members, with the Neah Bay being the largest community.

Homes: Long cedar planks were tied to upright poles that were secured in the ground, and these formed the walls of a **longhouse**. The roof was made of cedar planks that had a wide shallow groove in them. Each longhouse had as many as six separate living areas.

Food: The Makah subsisted mainly on sea mammals like whales and seals, fish, clams and oysters, but would also eat plants and land mammals like deer and bear if they were easily found.

Clothing: Makah men wore breech-cloths, while women wore short skirts made of cedar bark or grass. To keep off the frequent rains, they wore capes made of rushes, and in colder weather wore tunics, fur cloaks, and moccasins.

Art: The Makah carved art into many of their wooden objects, and are one of the Northwestern native groups who made totem poles to indicate family relationships or tell stories.

Roles: Traditionally, men were hunters and fishermen and sometimes went to war. Women gathered plants, herbs, and clams, and were responsible for most of the childcare and cooking.

Frontier towns sprouted after Washington became a territory.

Missionaries and Pioneers

Some people came to Washington not to make money but to "save souls." In 1836, missionary Marcus Whitman and his wife, Narcissa, set up a mission near Walla Walla. They wanted the Native Americans to convert to Christianity.

Many American settlers soon moved west along the Oregon Trail. Americans wanted all of the Oregon Country, and the dispute with Britain over control of the region became more heated. In 1846, the United States and Britain reached an agreement. In this agreement, the British gave up their claims to the land south of what was known as the 49th parallel (the imaginary line that represents 49 degrees north latitude). This line became the northern border of Washington. In return, the United States gave up its claims to the land north of the parallel.

American settlers continued to come into the territory. But the Native Americans did not want to give up their land. Some of them blamed the missionaries for bringing the settlers west. They also blamed the missionaries for bringing an epidemic of measles that killed many Cayuse children. A group of Cayuse led by Chief Tiloukaikt attacked the Walla Walla mission in 1847 and killed the Whitman family and eleven other people. This attack led to the Cayuse War. American soldiers soon defeated the Native Americans. Chief Tiloukaikt and the other warriors who had killed the Whitman party voluntarily surrendered. The chief and his warriors were hanged.

Wear Your Raincoat

If you visit the Olympic Peninsula, remember the rain forests there are among the rainiest places in the world. Places such as the Hoh Rain Forest are the only rain forests in the lower forty-eight states.

Washington Territory

The Oregon Territory was established by an act of Congress in 1848. It included all of present-day Oregon, Washington, and Idaho, as well as parts of Montana and Wyoming. More than one thousand settlers lived in the Washington region in 1850. By 1853, the population had expanded to nearly four thousand. These residents wanted their own territory, so a new act of Congress that year split off the region from the Oregon Territory and created the separate Washington Territory. The residents wanted to name the new territory Columbia, but the government decided to name it Washington, in honor of the first president.

The Washington Territory grew quickly. Part of this growth was a result of the success of the **logging** camps in the area. Two years before Washington became its own territory, the village of Seattle had been established near Puget Sound.

Chief Seattle of the Duwamish and Suquamish tribes was a friend to the settlers. But other native people felt threatened by them. The territory's governor, Isaac I. Stevens, met with tribal chiefs in 1855 to negotiate treaties. He proposed to buy Native American land in exchange for gifts and money. Many Native American leaders did not want to give up their land. In an attempt to save their land, these tribes went to war. By 1858, after three years of fighting, the U.S. Army had defeated the Native Americans. The U.S. government moved many Native Americans from their homelands and forced them to live on reservations.

Making a Folding Fan

Folding fans are an important part of Japan's history and culture. Many Japanese people brought these prized belongings to the state. Today, Japanese and Japanese Americans in Washington still treasure these traditional fans. By following these instructions, you can make your very own fan.

What You Need

One piece of printer paper

Markers

Ruler

Six 12-inch (30-cm) pipe cleaners

Adhesive tape

About 12 inches (30 cm) of narrow ribbon

What To Do

•   Fold the paper in half so it is 4 1/2 inches (11.4 cm) wide and 11 inches (28 cm) long. Decorate one side with markers, with the folded edge as the top. Many fans had pictures of gardens, with hanging trees, ponds, and small bridges.

•   Open the paper to the blank inside. Lay the

ruler along the 11-inch (28-cm) edge. Measure and mark every inch (2.5 cm) along this edge (ten marks). Do the same to the opposite edge. Using a dark marker, draw a line from the top mark to the opposite one on the bottom edge.

•   Fold the pipe cleaners in half. Starting with the first section, lay a folded pipe cleaner in every other section, between the lines. The pointy ends should face the top of the paper. Position the pipe cleaners so the points are all just a little bit lower than the fold in the paper. Tape the pipe cleaners to the paper. Close the paper by folding it in half again, over the pipe cleaners. The drawing you made should be facing you. Tape the left and right edges closed.

•   Now turn the paper over and look through the side without decorations. Find the line marking the first section. Make a fold there. At the next line, fold the paper the opposite way, so you are pleating the paper back and forth. Keep it up until you have made ten folds.

•   Thread the ribbon through the pipe cleaners at the bottom and tie it with a double knot. Trim or curl the ends of the ribbon, or tie a bow.

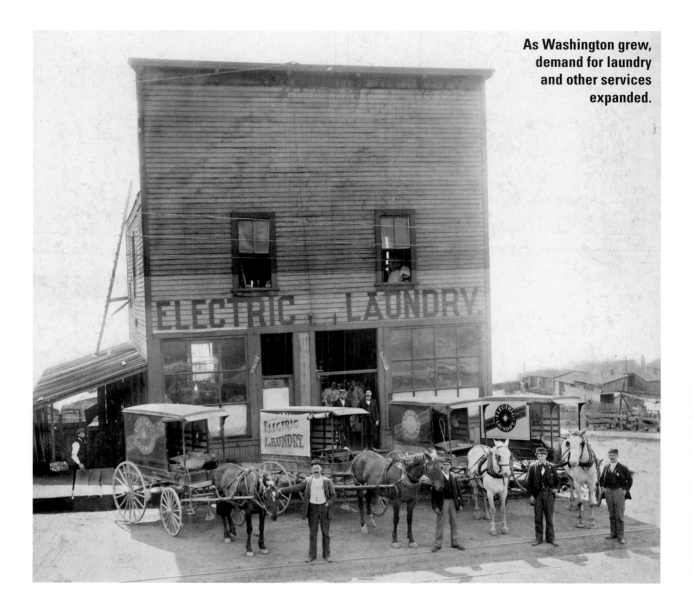

As Washington grew, demand for laundry and other services expanded.

Statehood

The settling of Washington by people from other parts of the United States was slow during the 1860s and 1870s. However, **immigrants** from other countries began to arrive at this time. Many Chinese immigrants came to the Washington area to prospect for gold, to work on building railroads, or to work in other businesses in the cities. American settlement again increased with the completion of railroad lines in the 1880s. People and goods could now get to the territory quickly and easily. In just ten years, between 1880 and 1890, the territory's population quadrupled. Americans from the East were moving to Washington. As a result of this growth in population, Washington officially became the forty-second state on November 11, 1889.

A Time of Growth

A series of gold rushes helped bring prosperity and more people to Washington. Gold was not discovered in the state, but in the late 1890s, many found riches in the Klondike region, which is located near Alaska in Canada. Thousands of prospectors heading for the gold fields of the Klondike were arriving in Seattle. Almost overnight, Seattle's population exploded. After stopping in Seattle, most prospectors moved north toward the gold. However, many stayed in Washington, impressed by its great scenic beauty and **economic** opportunities.

Industry and farming developed quickly in the early 1900s. Fishing became an important industry in the Puget Sound area. Apple orchards appeared across eastern Washington thanks to new irrigation systems that diverted water to fields used to grow crops. The timber industry became the biggest employer in the state. Shipbuilding also became an important industry. In 1904, the battleship USS *Nebraska* was launched from Moran Brothers shipyard in Seattle.

Crowds at left watch the launching of the USS Nebraska in October 1904.

Seattle used this poster to promote the Alaska-Yukon-Pacific Fair.

In 1909, Seattle held a huge fair that was called the Alaska-Yukon-Pacific Exposition. The fair included carnival rides and other forms of entertainment, as well as displays honoring Washington's history. The purpose of the fair was to celebrate the area's success and to attract more settlers and businesses to the Pacific Northwest. Nearly four million people attended the exposition.

While cities grew, many small towns and villages remained isolated. Communities farmed, fished, and ran their businesses, such as barber shops and restaurants. Hotels provided temporary housing for loggers and other workers.

Many of Washington's citizens worked in coal mines and logging camps. They worked in dangerous conditions for very little pay. New laws were passed to improve working conditions.

In 1854, Arthur Denny, one of the founders of Seattle, proposed a measure at the first session of the territorial legislature granting women the right to vote in the Washington Territory. It did not pass. Until the early twentieth century, women throughout most of the United States were not allowed to vote. In 1910, Washington became the fifth state to give women this right. Washington acted ten years before the Nineteenth Amendment to the U.S. Constitution gave women nationwide the right to vote. In 1926, Bertha Landes was elected mayor of Seattle. She was the first woman to be elected mayor of a major American city.

Tacoma

Vancouver

1. Seattle: population 608,660

Seattle is a major seaport city capitalizing on the safe harbor of a narrow isthmus between Puget Sound (an inlet of the Pacific Ocean) and Lake Washington. A major gateway for trade with Asia, it is the eighth largest port in the United States.

2. Spokane: population 208,916

Located on the Spokane River near the eastern border of Washington, about 20 miles (32 km) from Idaho, Spokane started as a trading post in 1810, and became an important rail and shipping center because of its location between mining and farming areas.

3. Tacoma: population 198,397

The neighboring deep-water harbor of this mid-sized port city on Puget Sound led the area to be chosen as the western end of the Northern Pacific Railroad in the late nineteenth century, which led to its motto, "When rails meet sails."

4. Vancouver: population 161,791

Vancouver is a city on the north bank of the Columbia River that was incorporated in 1857. The first permanent European settlement did not occur until 1824, when Fort Vancouver was established as a fur trading post.

5. Bellevue: population 122,363

Bellevue was founded in 1869 and the name was derived from a French term for "beautiful view." Seattle's largest suburb, Bellevue is home to the headquarters of many businesses, including technology companies that started in the 1990s.

6. Everett: population 103,019

Everett was founded in 1890 as an industrial and mining port and railroad stop. This industrial heritage can be seen in the Boeing Everett Factory, which is the largest building in the world in terms of interior space.

7. Kent: population 92,411

Kent was founded in the 1860s as Titusville. It capitalized on growing hops and lettuce, and was called "The Lettuce Capital of the World" during the 1930s. In the 1960s, Boeing and other aerospace and high-tech companies began building in Kent, changing the **economy**.

8. Yakima: population 91,067

Founded in 1886 as North Yakima, the name changed to simply Yakima in 1916. It is located in the Yakima Valley, a rich farming region where, as of 2011, 77 percent of all hops grown in the United States are produced.

9. Renton: population 90,927

A farming area since the 1860s, Renton became a city in 1901 with industries based in lumber production and coal mining. Industrial production increased during World War II, and continues. Other businesses like game producer Wizards of the Coast are headquartered there.

10. Spokane Valley: population 89,755

The City of Spokane Valley incorporated on March 31, 2003, but the first settler arrived in 1849. While the first settlers were farmers and silver miners, the area grew after railroads came through in the late 1800s.

Everett

Yakima

Spokane

Wars and Hard Time

During World War I (1914–1918), which the United States entered in 1917, more than sixty-eight thousand state residents served in the military. The United States government built Fort Lewis, one of the nation's largest army bases, in Pierce County.

When the Great Depression, a period of severe economic hardship, started in 1929, Washington's economy suffered. Four out of five lumber and paper mills closed. Tens of thousands of people lost their jobs. The federal government began a building program to improve lives and put people back to work. Huge dams were constructed on the Columbia River. These dams harnessed water power to produce electricity, prevented flooding, and created reservoirs to irrigate farmlands. The biggest was the Grand Coulee Dam, completed in 1941.

The Grand Coulee Dam has been called the "biggest thing built by the hands of man." It is nearly 1 mile (1.6 km) long. There is enough concrete in the dam to build a highway 60 feet (18 m) wide and 4 inches (10 cm) thick from Los Angeles to New York City.

Workers took nine years to build the Grand Coulee Dam, starting July 16, 1933.

Japanese-American families on the West Coast were sent to internment camps during World War II.

Behind the dam is Lake Roosevelt, which is 151 miles (243 km) long and stretches to the Canadian border. It took nine years to build the dam, which is the largest concrete structure in North America. It creates more electricity from water power than any other source in the nation.

World War II broke out in Europe in 1939. The United States entered the war after Japan attacked the U.S. naval base at Pearl Harbor in Hawaii on December 7, 1941. Washington's shipyards and aircraft manufacturers worked overtime to provide battleships and combat planes for the war. The electricity generated from the Grand Coulee Dam was especially helpful to the Washington industries that flourished during the war. In 1944, the Hanford Engineering Works in Richland became the top-secret site of plutonium production. It produced plutonium for some of the first atomic bombs. In August 1945, B-29 bombers produced by the Boeing Company in Seattle dropped atomic bombs on two Japanese cities. Japan surrendered by the next month, and the war ended.

World War II had especially devastating effects on the Japanese American population living on the West Coast. After the attack on Pearl Harbor, many Japanese Americans living in the United States were suspected of spying for—or at the least being loyal to—Japan. In most cases, there was little or no proof showing that Japanese Americans were spies or were disloyal. In 1942, President Franklin D. Roosevelt signed an executive order that led to the imprisonment of more than 100,000 men, women, and children of Japanese descent. Japanese Americans living in Washington, California, and Oregon were affected by this order. They were forced to sell most of their possessions. They had to abandon their businesses and leave their homes.

The Japanese Americans were moved to internment camps set up in isolated regions away from the coast. The camps were surrounded by barbed-wire fences and patrolled by armed guards. Approximately thirteen thousand Japanese Americans from Washington were sent to the camps. No internee was charged with or convicted of any act of espionage. People were placed in the camps without due process of law as required by the U.S. Constitution. They were forced to remain at these internment camps until shortly before the war ended in 1945.

Postwar Prosperity

After the war, Boeing began to build jets made specifically for transporting passengers. Washington's economy flourished. The government built a series of dams on the Columbia and Snake rivers that produced electrical power and helped with flood control and the irrigation of dry land.

World's fairs brought more people to Washington. In 1962, Seattle hosted Century 21, a world's fair. More than nine million people came to ride a futuristic monorail, to visit the Pacific Science Center, or to take in the view from the top of the Space Needle, a soaring

The World's Fair opened in Spokane on May 5, 1974.

605-foot (184.4-m) structure built especially for the fair. In 1974, Spokane had its own world's fair, called Expo '74. The fair's theme was a safe and clean environment. During the 1970s and 1980s, environmental cleanup became an important issue in the state. Washington was one of the first states in the country to start a recycling program.

Washington Today

Washington's population grew by almost 735,000 between 1980 and 1990, as new electronics and computer companies brought many jobs to the state. However,

The Space Needle has been a Seattle landmark since 1962.

by the beginning of the twenty-first century, Washington's economic boom had slowed. In early 2002, Washington and Oregon had the highest unemployment rates in the United States. Agricultural jobs in eastern Washington disappeared. As more people moved to the area, competition for jobs became stronger.

In 2008 and 2009, Washington's economy took more of a tumble. The United States was in a severe recession, and many of the state's largest employers laid off workers. In some ways, though, Washington was better off than other states. A large share of the state's income comes from trade. About one-quarter of the residents are involved in trading diverse goods with other states and countries. Many of these jobs remained stable during the tough economic times.

1. 1592

Greek explorer Juan de Fuca sails along the coast of what is now Washington.

2. November 15, 1805

Explorers Lewis and Clark reach the Pacific Ocean.

3. March 2, 1853

The Washington Territory splits from the Oregon Territory, which had been established in 1848. The Oregon Territory included what is now Washington, Oregon and Idaho, as well as parts of Montana and Wyoming.

4. October 21, 1872

Kaiser Wilhelm I of Germany resolves a dispute over ownership of the San Juan Islands between the United States and Great Britain. The islands were awarded to the U.S., setting the final boundary between it and Canada. The settlement ended what is called the Pig War because the only casualty was a pig.

5. September 8, 1883

The Northern Pacific railroad line between St. Louis and Tacoma is completed.

6. November 11, 1889

Washington becomes the forty-second state.

7. July 17, 1897

The announcement of large amounts of gold in northwestern Canada starts the Klondike Gold Rush, which turns Seattle into a boomtown.

8. March 22, 1941

The Grand Coulee Dam is formally dedicated. The dam is 5,223 feet (1,592 m) long, just 57 feet (17.4 m) short of a mile, and it is the largest concrete structure ever built.

9. May 18, 1980

Mount St. Helens, a volcanic mountain, erupts. More than 230 square miles (595.7 sq. km) of forest were blown down or scorched. The eruption lasted nine hours.

10. July 8, 2007

Boeing's Everett assembly factory unveils the Boeing 787 Dreamliner, the biggest, longest-range, and most fuel efficient wide-body airliner ever.

Seattle is a cultural melting pot.

The People

According to 2010 U.S. Census Bureau estimates, about 79 percent of Washington's population is white. Some of these residents are descendants of American and European settlers who came to the state many years ago. Others may be more recent immigrants from European countries such as Germany, Great Britain, Ireland, or the Scandinavian countries. People of Hispanic descent make up more than 11 percent of the population. Many of these residents are from Mexico. Asian Americans make up about 7 percent of the population. Almost 4 percent of Washingtonians are African American, and 1.5 percent of the population is Native American.

The First Residents

Native Americans were the first people to live in the region now known as Washington. Today, there are about 99,736 Native Americans living in Washington. Many of them live on more than twenty reservations across the state. Part of the Confederated Tribes of the Umatilla Indian reservation is found in the southeastern section of the state. This reservation is home to the Cayuse, Walla Walla, and Umatilla tribes. The Colville Indian reservation is in north-central Washington.

Who Washingtonians Are

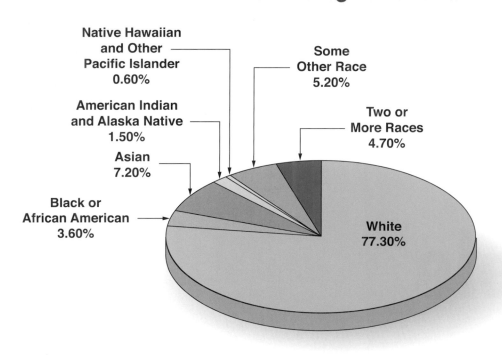

Native Hawaiian
and Other
Pacific Islander
0.60%

American Indian
and Alaska Native
1.50%

Asian
7.20%

Black or
African American
3.60%

Some
Other Race
5.20%

Two or
More Races
4.70%

White
77.30%

Total Population
6,724,540

Hispanic or Latino (of any race):

• 755,790 people (11.2%)

Note: The pie chart shows the racial breakdown of the state's population based on the categories used by the U.S. Bureau of the Census. The Census Bureau reports information for Hispanics or Latinos separately, since they may be of any race. Percentages in the pie chart may not add to 100 because of rounding.

Source: U.S. Bureau of the Census, 2010 Census

Fewer Native Americans, such as this member of the Umatilla tribe in 1910, were driven out of Washington than from most other states.

Children pick huckleberries on the Yakama Reservation.

The Yakama reservation spreads across more than one million acres (405,000 hectares) of protected land along the Cascade Mountains. It is one of the largest Native American reservations in the United States. The reservation is home to the Yakama Nation Museum and Cultural Center. The center houses a museum, restaurant, theater, research center, and library.

Many of Washington's Native American nations are interested in sharing their history and culture with others. Throughout the year, meetings and festivals are held across the state. Many Washington tribes, as well as tribes from other parts of the country, join in the festivities.

Asian Americans

Asian Americans have had a troubled history in Washington. In the 1870s and 1880s, many Chinese immigrants suffered when anti-Chinese riots destroyed their homes and businesses. Many American workers felt that these new immigrants were stealing their jobs. In 1885, a mob of Tacoma's leading citizens, including the mayor, forced Chinese residents to leave their homes. Many relocated to Portland, Oregon. In 1993, the Tacoma City Council passed a resolution to express regret for this poor treatment and the Chinese Reconciliation Project Foundation was founded in 1994 to educate the community about multicultural history and to celebrate their common qualities.

Before and during World War II, Washington's Japanese American residents also faced difficult times in the state. Takuji Yamashita was born in Japan but later moved to the United States and attended the University of Washington School of Law. In 1902, he graduated and passed

the bar exam with honors, but was not allowed to practice law. At that time, all attorneys had to be U.S. citizens, and federal law barred virtually all immigrants from Asia from becoming citizens. Unable to make a living as an attorney, Yamashita opened a restaurant. He later returned to Japan and died there in 1959. In 2001, the state supreme court declared Takuji Yamashita an honorary lawyer.

In Seattle, a Chinese American named Wing Luke became the first Asian American to hold an elected office in the state when he won a council seat in 1962. It was another sign that the state was moving away from its troubled history.

Today, the Asian American population in Washington is growing. Besides people of Chinese and Japanese heritage, there are many Vietnamese, Filipino, Laotian, Korean, Indian, and Thai Americans. In 1996, Gary Locke was elected governor of Washington, making him the first Chinese American state governor in the United States.

The Nordic Heritage Museum in Ballard opened in 1980.

A Slice of Scandinavia

Scandinavian immigrants settled the fishing and lumbering town of Ballard in the 1880s. In 1907, Ballard became part of Seattle, and today it is one of the city's most colorful and historic neighborhoods. Ballard's Nordic roots can be seen in its many businesses specializing in selling Scandinavian foods and gift items.

Education in Washington

When Washington was made a territory in 1853, American settlers had established only five schools in the region. Today, there are about two thousand public schools in the state and more than sixty places of higher learning. Whitman Seminary, named after the famous missionaries, was the first school of higher education to open—in 1859 in Walla Walla. It was renamed Whitman College in 1882. The University of Washington opened in 1861 in Seattle, and is one of the oldest universities on the West Coast. It is the largest university in the state. The school's sports teams are nicknamed the Huskies.

There are about two thousand public schools in Washington.

Bonnie J. Dunbar

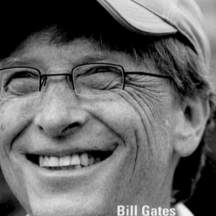

Bill Gates

Ben Haggerty

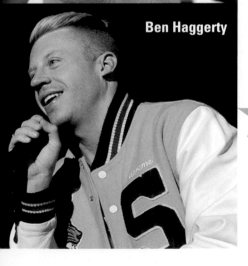

1. Bing Crosby

Born Harry Lillis Crosby in Tacoma in 1903, Bing Crosby was a famous singer and movie star. Crosby recorded more than one thousand songs, including "White Christmas," and won an Academy Award in 1944 for his role in the movie *Going My Way*.

2. Bonnie J. Dunbar

Born in Sunnyside in 1949, Dr. Dunbar worked for Boeing Computer Services and Rockwell International Space Division before starting at NASA in 1978 and becoming an astronaut in 1981. She is a veteran of five space flights.

3. Bill Gates

Bill Gates was born in Seattle in 1955. Gates and Paul Allen developed a computer language and founded the Microsoft Corporation. In 1987, at age thirty-one, Bill Gates became the youngest American self-made billionaire.

4. Ben Haggerty

Known professionally as Macklemore, Ben Haggerty was born in 1983 in Seattle. Collaborating with producer Ryan Lewis, their single "Thrift Shop" reached number one on the Billboard Hot 100 chart in 2013. They won four Grammy Awards in 2014, including Best New Artist.

5. Jolyn C. Heutmaker

Jolyn Heutmaker, known professionally as Josie Bissett, was born in Seattle in 1970. A model in print advertisements and television commercials since the age of twelve, she went on to star in the television series *Melrose Place*.

6. Hank Ketcham

The Seattle native wanted to be a cartoonist at an early age, and went to California to work as an animator, contributing to the Disney film *Bambi*. In 1951, his son Dennis became the inspiration for his comic strip, *Dennis the Menace*, which was later developed into a TV series and a movie.

7. Edward R. Murrow

Born in North Carolina but raised near Bellingham, Edward R. Murrow is a pioneer in television and radio news. He risked his life to broadcast from rooftops while London was bombed at the beginning of World War II.

8. Chief Seattle

Born in the 1780s, Chief Seattle was the leader of the Duwamish and Suquamish tribes. He made friends with the first white settlers and signed an important treaty, establishing two reservations for Native Americans.

9. Hope Solo

A two-time *Parade* All-American while a high-scoring soccer forward at Richland High School, Hope Solo was the goalkeeper for the U.S. women's teams that won gold medals at the 2008 and 2012 Summer Olympics.

10. Hilary Swank

Actress Hilary Swank was born in 1974 and grew up in Bellingham, where she was a Junior Olympian, and ranked fifth in the state in gymnastics. She has won more than thirty acting awards, including two Academy Awards and two Golden Globes.

Chief Seattle

Hope Solo

Hilary Swank

A Great Place to Live

From 1990 to 2000, the state's population increased by about one million. In 1990, it was the eighteenth state in population. In 2000, it ranked fifteenth. By 2010, the state had reached a population of more than 6.7 million and ranked thirteenth. About three out of every four Washingtonians live west of the Cascade Mountains. More than half of the state's population lives in the Puget Sound region. Many like its natural beauty, its mild climate, the friendly residents, and the different types of job opportunities.

Sports and Recreation

The people of Washington love to play and watch sports. Seattle is home to the Seahawks football team and the Seattle Storm women's basketball team. Safeco Field, home of Seattle's baseball team, the Mariners, was built in 1999 with a retractable roof and cost more than half a billion dollars.

The Seattle Storm, a WNBA team, is a vital part of Seattle's professional sports scene.

Olympic National Park is one of three national parks in Washington that draw hikers of all ages.

Hydroplane racing is a popular sport in Puget Sound. Every summer during Seattle's Seafair, thousands of locals and tourists come to watch the Unlimited Hydroplane Races on Lake Washington. These lightweight boats shoot across the water at speeds up to 200 miles (320 km) per hour.

Washington has three national parks. The largest is Mount Rainier National Park. Olympic National Park, in the far northwestern part of the state, is one of the most varied national parks in the country. Within its borders, it has rain forests, lakes,

Did You Know?

Mount Rainier, which is the highest point in Washington at 14,409 feet [4,392 m], was named after Peter Rainier. He was a British soldier who fought against the Americans in the Revolutionary War.

glaciers, and 57 miles (92 km) of untouched coastline. The state also boasts nine national forests, and more than one hundred state parks and historical sites. The other is North Cascades National Park.

Places to Visit

Washington is proud of its city parks as well as its national and state parks. Tacoma's Point Defiance Park is one of the largest city parks in the United States. Visitors can enjoy hiking trails, a zoo, a replica of a logging camp from the early 1900s, and Fort Nisqually, the first fur trading outpost on Puget Sound of the Hudson's Bay Company. Manito Park in Spokane has a number of colorful flowering gardens, including a Japanese garden. Riverfront Park is just as impressive. It features waterfalls from the Spokane River and some of the attractions from Expo '74, including the U.S. Pavilion.

Roses provide a canopy at Tacoma's Point Defiance Park.

The Experience Music Project/ Science Fiction Museum and Hall of Fame houses many innovative galleries and hands-on exhibits.

Seattle is proud of its many fine museums. The Burke Museum of Natural History and Culture is located on the University of Washington campus. The Seattle Asian Art Museum has one of the best collections of Asian art in the country. The Museum of Flight has more than fifty aircraft on display. Among them are the first presidential jet and an Apollo space command module. The Seattle Aquarium has an Underwater Dome that holds 400,000 gallons (1.5 million liters) of water. The Experience Music Project/Science Fiction Museum and Hall of Fame is devoted to the history and exploration of popular music and science fiction.

Tacoma is the home of the Washington State History Museum, which includes a special interactive section of hands-on exhibits. There are also many other museums across the state. The World Kite Museum and Hall of Fame is in Long Beach. Visitors who want to learn more about Lewis and Clark can go to the Lewis and Clark Interpretive Center in Fort Canby State Park.

Active Volcanoes

There are five major volcanoes in the Cascade Range in Washington: Mount Baker, Glacier Peak, Mount Rainier, Mount Adams, and Mount St. Helens.

10 KEY EVENTS ★ ★

Cherry Blossom and Japanese Cultural Festival

Great Bavarian Ice Fest

Jules Fest

1. Cherry Blossom and Japanese Cultural Festival

This annual event takes place in April in Seattle and celebrates Japanese art and culture in the Pacific Northwest. The festival was founded in the mid-1970s in appreciation for the gift of one thousand cherry trees to Seattle by the Japanese government in commemoration of the country's bicentennial (two hundredth anniversary).

2. Ellensburg Rodeo

Started in September 1923, the Ellensburg Rodeo is one of the most popular rodeos in the country. Members of the Yakama Indian Nation start off each evening's events with a traditional dance in the arena.

3. Great Bavarian Ice Fest

This winter festival in Leavenworth is held in January and features dogsled rides, a snowshoe race, and an ice-cube hunt for children. Another highlight is the Northwest Regional Dog Sled Pulling Competition.

4. Jules Fest

In December, this Norwegian holiday tradition in Poulsbo features a local girl dressed as the Lucia Bride, who lights the Christmas tree. She is followed by Santa Claus, who listens as the children tell him what they want for Christmas.

5. Port Townsend Blues and Heritage Festival

Every summer, leading blues musicians and singers gather in Port Townsend to perform and conduct musical workshops.

6. Seafair

The biggest community festival in the Pacific Northwest, Seafair takes place from early July through early August in Seattle. Popular events include a milk carton derby, a torchlight parade, and the famed Unlimited Hydroplane Races on Lake Washington.

7. Upper Skagit Bald Eagle Festival

In late January or early February, thousands of people travel to the Upper Skagit River Valley to see one of the largest winter gatherings of bald eagles in the country. Visitors can also attend lectures, storytelling, and music concerts.

8. Washington State Apple Blossom Festival

Held in April in Wenatchee, this eleven-day festival has parades, a scholarship auction, and a children's art contest and exhibition.

9. Western Washington State Fair

Sometimes called the Puyallup Fair, this is one of the ten largest fairs in North America. It runs for seventeen days every September. Visitors can enjoy rides, concerts, livestock shows, and rodeos—and kids can even test their skills at riding sheep.

10. Yakama Treaty Days

This Native American celebration is held every June to commemorate the anniversary of the signing of the 1855 treaty. Toppenish is located in the Yakama Indian Reservation in southeast Washington.

Apple Blossoms

Western Washington State Fair

Lawmakers meet in the State Capitol in Olympia.

How the Government Works

The basic structure of Washington's government, as well as rules about how government operates and what it can or cannot do, are established by the state constitution. It was created in 1889, when Washington became a state. This constitution has been amended, or revised, over the years, but it remains the foundation of government in the state.

The center of Washington's state government is Olympia, the state capital. In addition to its state government, Washington has many local governments. The state is divided into thirty-nine counties. Most of these counties are governed by a board of county commissioners. The three commissioners in each county are assisted by a number of other officials. They include a county clerk, a treasurer, and a sheriff. There are 281 cities and towns in Washington. Most of them are governed by a mayor and a city council. The elected mayors and council members serve four-year terms. Some cities in Washington are run by a city manager instead of a mayor.

The Capital

Olympia was named Washington's capital when Washington became a territory in 1853. It is located at the southern end of Puget Sound. It was known by different names to the Native Americans who lived there for many generations and to the first European settlers.

It was renamed for the Olympic Mountains northwest of the city. Olympia has about 45,000 people and is considered a small capital city. The governor's residence is located in Olympia. The building where lawmakers meet, the Temple of Justice building where the supreme court hears cases, and the beautiful grounds with Japanese cherry trees are often called the Capitol Campus.

Branches of Government

EXECUTIVE

The executive branch includes the governor, lieutenant governor, secretary of state, treasurer, and attorney general. The governor is head of the executive branch. He or she either approves or rejects laws passed by the legislature. The governor also makes up the state budget each year and appoints officials to government departments and agencies. Elected officials in the executive branch serve four-year terms. They do not have a limit on the number of terms they can serve.

LEGISLATIVE

Washington's legislature, or lawmaking body, is called the general assembly. It is made up of two houses. The house of representatives has ninety-eight members. The state senate has forty-nine members. Members of the house of representatives serve two-year terms and may not serve more than six of the previous twelve years. Members of the senate serve four-year terms and cannot hold office for more than eight of the previous fourteen years. No legislator can serve in the general assembly for more than fourteen of the previous twenty years.

Visitors can tour the beautiful State Capitol.

Legislators propose and pass laws for the state. Any proposed law must be passed by a majority vote in both houses of the legislature before it goes to the governor for executive approval.

JUDICIAL

The judicial branch interprets and enforces the laws of the state. Washington's court system ranges from municipal (city), district (county), and superior (state) courts up to the state supreme court. When a defendant or plaintiff first protests, or appeals, the outcome of a case in municipal, district, or superior court, the case goes to a court of appeals, which can uphold or overturn a lower court's rulings. Court of appeals decisions may be further appealed to the highest state court—the supreme court. The supreme court is made up of nine judges who are elected to serve six-year terms. Judges for the court of appeals are also elected to serve six-year terms. District court judges are elected to four-year terms. Municipal court and superior court judges can be elected or appointed to serve four-year terms.

How a Bill Becomes a Law

Did you ever wonder how state laws are made? Citizens in Washington can play a key part in this decision making. If a citizen has an idea for a law, he or she can suggest it to representatives in the general assembly. Sometimes voters will collect many signatures from other voters who share their opinions on an idea. Then they present this petition about a proposed law to legislators. Members of the general assembly also come up with ideas for new laws.

The senate's page program gives young people a look at Washington's government in action.

A proposed law is called a bill. Wherever the idea originates, a representative or person on the representative's staff takes the idea and actually writes a bill. A bill can be introduced first in the house of representatives or in the senate. If the bill starts in the house of representatives, the president of the house of representatives assigns a committee to review the bill.

The members of the committee hold hearings and discuss the bill. If they agree that it should be a law, they send it back to the house of representatives. The entire house of representatives then votes on the bill. If the bill is approved by a majority vote, it is sent to the state senate. The senate follows a procedure similar to the one in the house of representatives. A committee considers the bill, and if it is approved by the committee, then the entire senate votes on whether to approve it.

When both parts of the legislature have approved a bill, it is sent to the governor. If the governor approves, the bill becomes a law. However, if the governor rejects—or vetoes— the bill, the house and senate still have a chance to pass it. If the house and senate both vote in favor of the bill again—this time by a two-thirds majority—the governor's veto can be overturned, and the bill becomes a law.

★ 1. Henry 'Scoop' Jackson: Congressman and Senator, 1941-1983

The Everett native was the chairman of the Committee on Indian Affairs, the chairman of the Democratic National Committee in 1960, and twice ran unsuccessfully for his party's nomination for president. He was posthumously awarded the Presidential Medal of Freedom in 1984.

★ 2. Gary Locke: State Representative, 1983-94; and Governor, 1997-2005

The first Chinese-American governor in the U.S., Gary Locke was born in Seattle in 1950. Locke was also appointed U.S. Secretary of Commerce in 2009 by President Barack Obama and served as United States Ambassador to China until February 2014.

★ 3. Dixy Lee Ray: Governor, 1976-1981

Washington's first woman governor, Dixy Lee Ray was born in Tacoma in 1914. In 1973, she headed the U.S. Atomic Energy Commission (AEC). Ray was enthusiastic but also cautious about nuclear power. She also hosted a local television program called "Animals of the Sea."

WASHINGTON
YOU CAN MAKE A DIFFERENCE

★ Contacting Lawmakers

For information about the governor and how to contact the governor, visit:

www.governor.wa.gov

For names, phone numbers and email addresses for local Washingtonian legislators, visit the following site and click on the area of the map in which you live:

www.leg.wa.gov/pages/home.aspx

To find out who represents an area in the federal government in Washington D.C. as a congressman or senator, visit:

app.leg.wa.gov/DistrictFinder/?congress=1

★ Getting Involved

Many legislators have individual websites or Facebook pages so that they can keep in touch with the people they represent (called their constituents). It is important to let your state and federal representatives know how you feel about issues that they will be deciding on, or they might not represent you and your district correctly.

Sometimes kids can help make new laws, too. In 1997, a group of students from Crestwood Elementary School in Kent, Washington, suggested to state legislators that Washington should have a state insect. The legislature agreed to allow school students to decide what the state insect should be. About twenty-five thousand students from more than one hundred school districts voted. They chose the green darner dragonfly, which is also called the mosquito hawk. The students voted for this insect because it can be found all over Washington and helps by eating insect pests such as mosquitoes. In 1997, the common green darner dragonfly was officially proclaimed the state insect of Washington.

That is just one example of how young Washingtonians can take part in their government. By staying informed about local issues and current events, you can decide how you would like to help. Volunteering for a campaign or spending some time helping groups who are trying to have a bill passed are just two of the many ways you can help your community.

Farmers grow an abundance of produce, especially in central Washington.

Making a Living

Washington has a varied economy. Plentiful rainfall or good irrigation systems, as well as rich soil, make much of the state perfect for farming. The western region's mild climate has attracted many businesses to this corner of America. A number of large companies have made their headquarters in Washington. Boeing, one of the world's largest producers of airplanes, has locations in Bellevue, Everett, Issaquah, Kent, Renton, Seattle, Spokane, and other cities. The headquarters for the Costco warehouse store chain is in Issaquah. Redmond is the base for the computer software giant Microsoft. Seattle is home to the Nordstrom department-store chain, the Starbucks Coffee Company, and the online retailer Amazon.com.

Riches from the Earth

Washington is first when it comes to many farm products. The state produces more pears, sweet cherries, red raspberries, lentils, and hops than any other state. The hop plant is used in making beer, medicines, and other products. Washington is second among the states in the production of potatoes, peas, apricots, and asparagus. Most of the fruits and vegetables are grown in central Washington. This region was once too dry for growing crops, but irrigation turned it into fertile farmland. The dry air cuts down on insect pests that threaten fruit trees.

Washington's orchards grow more apples than those in any other state.

The first apples arrived in Washington on a sailing ship in 1825, and pioneers were soon growing apple trees from the seeds. The first commercial apple orchards appeared around 1889. Today, there are more than 225,000 acres (91,055 ha) of apple orchards in central Washington. About ten billion to twelve billion apples are handpicked in Washington State orchards each year amounting to around six billion pounds (2.7 billion kg) of apples, more than any other state. Most of these apples are grown in the eastern foothills of the Cascade Mountains. The soil there is rich in lava ash, which is good for growing crops, and there is plenty of sunshine and cool mountain water.

There is a good chance that the flower bulbs many Americans plant each fall came from Washington. Tulip, iris, and other flower bulbs are cultivated there and then shipped across the country.

Dairy farms flourish in western Washington. There are also many cattle and sheep ranches in the eastern part of the state, where the flat grasslands are perfect for grazing.

Mining is another important part of the state's economy. Washington's most important mineral is coal. Most of the coal mines are located in the southwestern part of the state. Other minerals mined in Washington include magnesium, zinc, limestone, sand and gravel, and silver.

Logging was one of the first industries in Washington. The state's great forests are still being harvested. Some of the logs are taken to mills where they are cut into lumber for building. Other mills turn wood into paper products. The only states that produce more lumber are California and Oregon.

Gardeners across the country plant bulbs that originated in Washington.

★ 10 KEY INDUSTRIES ★

Agriculture

1. Agriculture

Washington is the leading producer of sweet cherries in the country, and black and yellow cherries are also grown. The dry climate in the central part of the state has allowed Washington to lead the U.S. in apple production for nearly 100 years.

2. Bitcoin Mining

Bitcoin is digital currency that is mined by computers that solve **cryptographic** equations or codes. Washington has some of the country's lowest rates for electricity, which computers need a lot of to do this work. Dell, Yahoo, Microsoft, and Intuit run data centers in Grant County.

3. Construction

Washington's population increased by more than 50 percent from 1980 to 2010, creating a lot of work in building new houses and buildings for businesses. This industry accounts for about six percent of all jobs statewide.

Construction

4. Fishing

The primary wild species caught in Grays Harbor, Willapa Bay, and Puget Sound are salmon, halibut, cod, and herring, although crab are also brought in. Salmon, trout, and shellfish are also farm raised for harvest.

5. Forestry

Lumber continues be a primary product of Washington as it is one of the country's leading producers of softwood lumber and plywood. The state's timberlands have the highest per-acre yield in the country.

Fishing

6. Health Care

The biggest employer in the state is the health care industry, accounting for nearly 16 percent of all jobs, including doctors, nurses, health care aides, and those working in retirement homes.

7. Manufacturing

Electronics such as computer microchips, phones and wireless communications equipment, and transportation products—planes, trucks, and ships—are among the goods made here. Boeing, one of the world's top aircraft producers, has half of its workforce in Washington.

8. Power Generation

The hundreds of dams that block the Columbia and other rivers in western Washington generate one-third of all the hydroelectric power in the United States. The Grand Coulee Dam is among the largest power plants in the world.

9. Technology

With computer giant Microsoft headquartered in Redmond, Washington has the highest concentration of high-tech jobs of any state in the country (11.4 percent). The state is also home to the largest online shopping company in the United States, Amazon.com.

10. Tourism

The state brings in billions of tourist dollars each year as people come to ski and hike its mountains, walk its rain forests and visit its three national parks. This keeps a lot of Washingtonians employed.

Hydroelectric Power

Technology

Tourism

Recipe for Applesauce

Washington is known for its delicious apples. Why not make them into applesauce? This treat can be served warm or cold, and stores well in the refrigerator.

What You Need

10 apples (peeled, cored, and sliced)

1 cup (237 milliliters) apple cider (or apple juice or water)

juice of one lemon

½ cup (118 mL) brown sugar

½ teaspoon (2.5 mL) cinnamon

1/8 tsp (.6 mL) ground cloves (optional)

1/8 tsp (.6 mL) ground nutmeg (optional)

1/8 tsp (.6 mL) ground allspice (optional)

What to Do

• Wash and dry the apples. Peel and core them, then cut them into ½ inch (1.3 cm) slices.

• Add the cider (or juice or water) and lemon juice as soon as possible, to keep the cut apples from turning brown.

• Add the spices to taste. The optional spices will make the applesauce more flavorful, and amounts can be adjusted to your own tastes.

• Put the mixture into a saucepan and cook over a medium heat for at least 30 minutes, stirring continually (if you have a slow cooker, you can leave them in there for several hours on low heat with no stirring).

• Mash the cooked apples with a potato masher, or puree them in a food processor.

• Now, enjoy it!

Wealth From the Sea

Washingtonians love their salmon—baked, broiled, or marinated. No state except Alaska catches and packages more of this delicious, pink-fleshed fish. There are more than two hundred other edible fish and shellfish caught in Pacific coastal waters and inland rivers. Commercial fishing provides the state with millions of dollars each year.

The oyster beds near Olympia are among the finest in North America. The Olympia oyster is a Washington delicacy. These small oysters are about 2 inches (5 cm) across. Razor clams are another favorite. Thousands of clam diggers come to beaches to dig up these clams. But there is a fifteen-razor-clam limit. Digging for razor clams can be a challenge because, unlike most other clams, the razor clam can "run away." It elongates its body out of its shell and burrows deep down in the sand.

Fishermen's Terminal at the Port of Seattle is a great place to buy fresh fish.

Making Things

Almost 227,000 workers in the state are employed in manufacturing. The biggest industry is the manufacturing of transportation equipment, especially aircraft and equipment for aerospace travel. Nearly one-third of these workers are employed by the Boeing Company. The Boeing plant in Everett covers 60 acres (24 ha) and is ten stories high. It is one of the largest enclosed spaces in the world. It has to be large enough to fit the wide-body jumbo passenger jets that are assembled there.

The shipbuilding industry is centered in Seattle, Bremerton, and Tacoma. Other important goods made in Washington include paper, industrial machinery, precision instruments, and printed materials like brochures and newspapers.

Computer software, data storage, and other high-tech companies have become big business in Washington in the past thirty years. In addition to Microsoft's headquarters in Redmond, the state hosts several other companies in the computer and technology industries. Bothell hosts Lockheed Martin Aculight, which creates lasers. Seattle is home to two research and development offices for Google, as well as an office for Adobe software developers.

Boeing builds airplanes in one of the largest enclosed spaces in the world.

At the Pike Place Fish Market, where salmon are tossed, you can make the catch of the day.

Tourist Dollars

Washington's natural beauty and its many other attractions make it a top state for **tourism**. In 2013, the tourism industry earned about $17.6 billion. There is even an Academy of Hospitality and Tourism program in some high schools in Seattle. Students learn about the tourism industry and job opportunities in that field. They study travel subjects and go on field trips.

Visitors come to take in the sights and experience all that the state has to offer. The tourism industry also keeps many Washingtonians employed.

Trading Goods

Washington's export trade is very important to the state economy. Exports are goods that are sent from one source to other places. According to the Department of Commerce, Washington exported more than $81.9 billion worth of goods in 2013. The state is the fourth largest exporter in the country. Washington exports items such as computer software, transportation and aerospace materials, electronic and scientific equipment, wood products, and crops. Washington's location plays a major part in its international exporting success.

Washington also sends goods to its neighboring states and other states across the country. The same trade routes allow the state to import, or bring in, goods from other places.

From Washington's ports, products can be exported around the world.

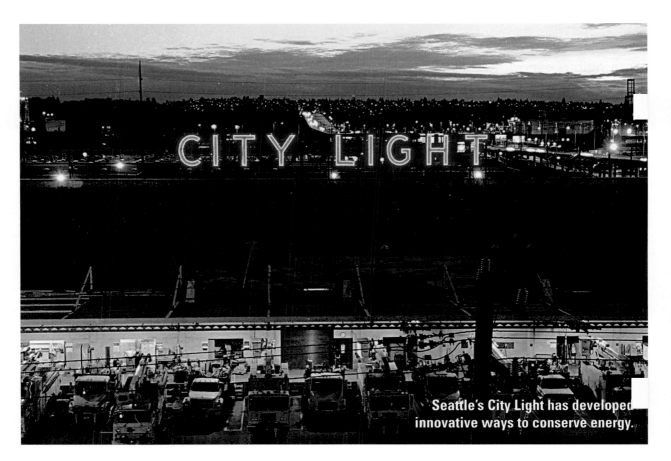

Seattle's City Light has developed innovative ways to conserve energy.

What Does the Future Hold?

Running the complex machines of Washington's many industries requires a great deal of energy. Washington's power companies are at the forefront of finding new ways to save energy and to produce electricity using new technologies that do not cause pollution. Seattle City Light, the power company for Seattle, has become well known for its efforts in energy conservation. How do this company and other energy companies conserve so much energy? One way is by, in effect, paying consumers to use less electricity. Avista Utilities in Spokane is giving its customers rebates when they buy energy-efficient equipment. Another way is by letting people pay less for electricity when they use it during low-demand times, such as at night. Washington's energy companies produce electricity using wind and water power, which do not cause air pollution, and they encourage customers to install solar panels. In most cases, the companies will pay customers for "extra" electricity—generated by solar panels—which customers do not need for themselves and send to their power company.

Innovative ideas and the hard work of dedicated Washingtonians continue to prepare the state for the future, in the twenty-first century and beyond.

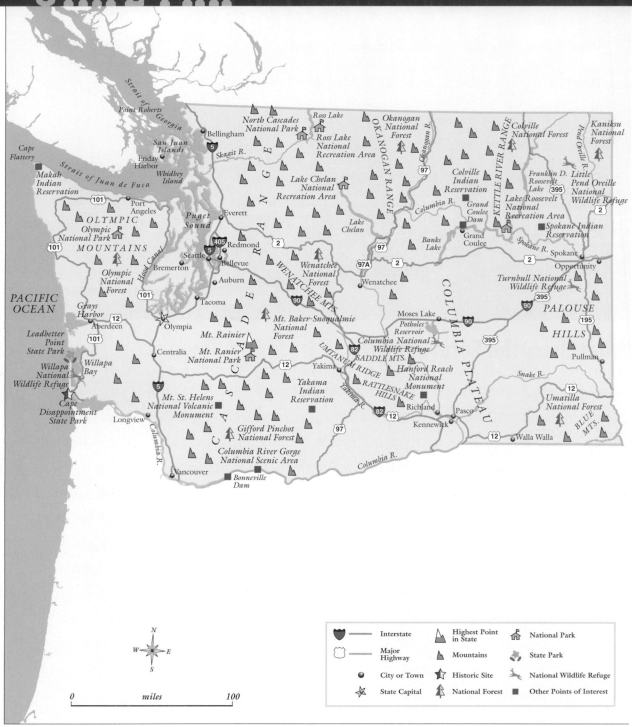

Strait of Georgia

Point Roberts

Cape
Flattery

Makah
Indian
Reservation

Strait of Juan de Fuca

San Juan
Islands

Friday
Harbor

Bellingham

Skagit R.

North Cascades
National Park

Ross Lake

Ross Lake
National
Recreation
Area

Okanogan
National
Forest

Colville
National Forest

Kaniksu
National
Forest

Whidbey
Island

Port
Angeles

OLYMPIC

Olympic
National Park

MOUNTAINS

Everett

Puget
Sound

Redmond

Seattle

Bellevue

Bremerton

Auburn

Olympic
National
Forest

Hood Canal

Lake Chelan
National
Recreation
Area

Lake
Chelan

Wenatchee
National
Forest

Wenatchee

Colville
Indian
Reservation

Columbia R.

Grand
Coulee
Dam

Banks
Lake

Grand
Coulee

Franklin D.
Roosevelt
Lake

Little
Pend Oreille
National
Wildlife Refuge

Lake Roosevelt
National
Recreation
Area

Pend Oreille R.

Spokane Indian
Reservation

Spokane R.

Spokane

Opportunity

Turnbull National
Wildlife Refuge

PACIFIC
OCEAN

Grays
Harbor

Aberdeen

Leadbetter
Point
State Park

Willapa
National
Wildlife Refuge

Willapa
Bay

Cape
Disappointment
State Park

Olympia

Tacoma

Centralia

Mt. Rainier

Mt. Ranier
National Park

Mt. St. Helens
National Volcanic
Monument

Longview

Gifford Pinchot
National Forest

Columbia River Gorge
National Scenic Area

Vancouver

Columbia R.

Bonneville
Dam

Mt. Baker-Snoqualmie
National
Forest

Yakima

Yakama
Indian
Reservation

Yakima R.

UMTANUM RIDGE

SADDLE MTS.

RATTLESNAKE
HILLS

Columbia National
Wildlife Refuge

Hanford Reach
National
Monument

Moses Lake

Potholes
Reservoir

COLUMBIA PLATEAU

Richland

Pasco

Kennewick

Snake R.

Walla Walla

Umatilla
National Forest

BLUE
MTS.

PALOUSE

HILLS

Pullman

Columbia R.

CASCADE RANGE

WENATCHEE MTS.

OKANOGAN RANGE

KETTLE RIVER RANGE

	Interstate		Highest Point in State		National Park
	Major Highway		Mountains		State Park
	City or Town		Historic Site		National Wildlife Refuge
	State Capital		National Forest		Other Points of Interest

N
W E
S

0   miles   100

1. What mountain range is Mount St. Helens located in?

2. What bodies of water intrude on the northwestern corner of Washington?

3. Which national wildlife refuge is located outside of Spokane?

4. What major highway runs across the central part of the state?

5. The Blue Mountains are located near what city?

6. What is the name of the Indian reservation southwest of Yakima?

7. What U.S. highway would you take to go from Spokane to Moses Lake?

8. State Route 195 connects what two cities?

9. What water feature is near Moses Lake?

10. Kennewick is located near what river?

Puget Sound

Turnbull National Wildlife Refuge

1. Cascade Range
2. Puget Sound, Strait of Juan de Fuca, and Strait of Georgia
3. Turnbull National Wildlife Refuge
4. State Highway 2
5. Pullman or Walla Walla
6. Yakama Indian Reservation
7. Interstate
8. Spokane and Pullman
9. Potholes Reservoir
10. Snake River

State Flag, Seal, and Song

The state flag is green with the official state seal in the center.

Washington's state seal is a portrait of George Washington. The words, "The Seal of the State of Washington" are printed around the portrait. The year that Washington became a state, 1889, is at the bottom.

The state song is "Washington My Home," with words and music by Helen Davis. It was adopted March 19, 1959.

To learn the lyrics, visit:

www.50states.com/songs/washingt.htm#.U3JVuJtwq8A

Glossary

climate   The average weather conditions of a particular place or region over a period of years.

cryptographic   Pertaining to the art of writing or solving codes.

dam   A barrier preventing the flow of water, which may or may not generate electrical power.

economy   he way an system of production, trade, and ownership is arranged.

glaciers   Large bodies of ice moving slowly down a slope or valley or spreading outward on land surface.

immigrants   People who come to a country to live there.

industry   The businesses that provide a particular product or service or manufacturing activity.

logging   To cut trees for lumber or to clear land of trees in lumbering.

longhouse   A long dwelling for several families.

manufacturing   To make into a product suitable for use from raw materials by hand or by machinery.

population   The whole number of people living in a country or region.

reservation   An area lands so reserved especially for use by Native Americans to continue to live by tribal laws and rights as per federal government treaties.

settlers   People who move into a new region and stay.

tourism   The practice of traveling for pleasure or the business of encouraging and serving such traveling.

More About Washington

BOOKS

Downey, Tika. *Washington: The Evergreen State*. New York, NY: Rosen Publishing, 2010.

Issacs, Sally. *Bill and Melinda Gates*. Mankato, MN: Heinemann-Raintree, 2009.

Riley, Gail Blasser. *Volcano! The 1980 Mount St. Helens Eruption*. New York, NY: Bearport Publishing, 2006.

McWhorter, Lucullus Virgil. *Yellow Wolf: His Own Story*. Caldwell, ID: Caxton Press, 2008.

WEBSITES

Official State of Washington Homepage:

www.access.wa.gov

The Washington State Historical Society:

www.wshs.org

The Washington State Senate Page Program:

www.leg.wa.gov/senate/administration/pageprogram/Pages/default.aspx

ABOUT THE AUTHOR

Steven Otfinoski has written more than ninety fiction and nonfiction books for young readers. His previous works for Cavendish Square include books on states, history, and animals.

Tea Benduhn writes books and edits a magazine. She lives in the beautiful state of Wisconsin with her husband and two cats.

Hex Kleinmartin, PhD, has taught anthropology, archaeology, and history, and has written several books and papers on these subjects.

Index

Index